ME,
AN AUTHOR?

Also by April O'Leary

Ride the Wave: Journey to Peaceful Living

The Ultimate Love Affair: Awaken
to God's Love in Just 40 Days

The Old Cocoon

Sober Moms, Happy Moms: 12 Real-Life
Stories of Women Who Gave Up Alcohol
and Found a Better Way

WHO ME,
AN AUTHOR?

If *THEY* can do it,
so can YOU!

APRIL O'LEARY
Founder of O'Leary Publishing

NAPLES, FL

Published in the United States by O'Leary Publishing

www.olearypublishing.com

ISBN (print): 978-1-952491-84-9

ISBN (ebook): 978-1-952491-85-6

Cataloging–in–Publication Data is on file with the Library of Congress.

Editing by Heather Davis Desrocher

Proofreading by Boris Boland

Cover and Interior Design by Jessica Angerstein

Printed in the United States of America

May you have the courage to say YES
to the book that is inside of you.

Contents

The Power of Your Pen

As the old saying goes, "The pen is mightier than the sword." Books educate, inspire and change the world. They encourage new ways of thinking and help evolve industries. They are tools for reaching farther and wider than one human could do on their own. Books are powerful and your pen can channel this power, too!

I'm so glad you're considering writing a book. I'm April O'Leary, the founder of O'Leary Publishing, and we help first-time authors share their message in a way that is personal, yet professional. We often take our aspiring authors from idea to publication, helping them craft their message and reach their readers in a way that makes a lasting impact.

There is nothing more fulfilling to me than the privilege of working with new and returning authors to help them put their inspiring, educational and transformational works out into the world. Our team takes great pride in the editorial process, the custom book design, the strategic book launch, and the full-scale author branding that we have done for so many of our authors. We can do that for you, too. Let's begin!

Take the Author Adventure Quiz

Have you ever had that nagging thought, *I should write a book someday*? Maybe friends and family keep telling you it's something you absolutely must do. If you have unique skills, experiences, or knowledge that could help others, sharing your ideas in a book is an amazing way to pay it forward, elevate your voice and grow your business. You'll also be adding to the expanding knowledge base in your industry or possibly even leaving a legacy for your family. But maybe you're thinking, *Who am I to write a book?*

The good news is that most of us feel that way before we put pen to paper. We discount our message or knowledge because we assume others are more credentialed or qualified to write our book. Or we think that our experiences are not rich enough or important enough to share. But who are the anonymous *THEYs* that are more qualified, more skilled, or more important than YOU?

Stop and think about it. Who specifically is that person in your life that you feel is more qualified to write about your experience than you? Is it a colleague who has published more articles in more respected journals? A business leader who has decades more experience? An entrepreneur who has a larger following online? A friend who has overcome more difficult circumstances? Who are *THEY*?

Let me set the record straight, *THEY* don't exist. Nope. *THEY* don't have your thoughts, your heart, or your unique mix of experiences that have shaped you up to this very moment. So, just this once, I want you to focus solely on YOU. Forget all those doubts about not being qualified to write a book – even if it's just for a minute – and dive into the Author Adventure quiz.

Read the following ten statements. Circle the ones that are true for you.

1 I have professional expertise or knowledge that could help others.

2 I have overcome some difficult personal circumstances that could inspire others.

3 I want to enhance my public speaking opportunities, professionally or personally.

4 I want to enhance or pivot in my career.

5 I want a strategic marketing tool for my career.

6 I want to share professional lessons with future leaders.

7 I am passionate about enhancing the visibility of a nonprofit or cause.

8 I have a social media following and they are curious to know more.

9 I want to inspire others along their spiritual journey.

10 I want to leave a legacy for future generations.

If you circled:

None of the statements above	NO - This is not the book for you
One of the statements	MAYBE - You might want to consider becoming an author
Two or more	YES - Keep reading. The world needs YOU!

To complete the full Author Adventure Quiz for FREE on our website, scan the code below or visit www.olearypublishing.com.

This short guide is broken into two sections: WHY and HOW.

Understanding the WHY behind your actions is the key to making a meaningful impact. That's why the first section dives into the WHYs of writing a book. Here, you'll discover inspiring stories from real people – just like you – who took the leap to become authors. And they're not just any authors; they're proud O'Leary Publishing authors. Each author represents one of the ten reasons to write a book. Feel free to jump to the authors who represent the reasons you circled on the previous page and read about their adventures to authorhood.

I speak with aspiring authors on a regular basis who are confused about book publishing. Should they get a literary agent? Will the publisher make them a New York Times Best Selling author? HOW does it work?! Understanding even the basics of HOW to do something can significantly lessen the fear of giving it a try. Seeing HOW someone else succeed gives me confidence that I can do the same! That's the essence of the second section – it offers a high-level overview of the publishing process. I'll walk you through the steps of how to transform your idea into a polished manuscript. I even include a link so you can speak with me personally!

By the time you finish this book, I hope you'll be ready to take the first steps toward becoming an author. The world needs to hear your voice. Our team is here to help you, every step of the way.

PART

(1)

Why You?

I was that child who constantly asked "WHY?" – much to my mother's chagrin. One Christmas, she even gifted me a book titled *When Do Fish Sleep...and Other Imponderables of Everyday Life* by David Feldman because I wanted to understand everything. And yes, I'm still that curious today.

Asking "WHY" is a natural part of being human. It helps us understand our world and keeps us curious and adventurous. That's exactly why I begin this book by encouraging you to explore WHY you should become an author. It is an adventure, to be sure; but without a clear purpose, crossing the finish line can feel too long and difficult.

I have found that hearing the stories of people who have already accomplished something I want to accomplish makes my dream feel possible... and dare I say, likely!

In the following pages, you will meet some of our authors, who said "YES" to the same statements you circled in the Author Adventure Quiz on page 5. You will hear their stories and you can connect with them online. I've included their names, websites, and book titles. They are real people – just like you!

Let's go through the ❿ statements from the Author Adventure Quiz, in order. I'll introduce you to 10 new authors who have successfully written and launched their books for the same reasons you circled on page 5.

❶ I have professional expertise or knowledge that could help others.

Paul Arciero, PhD, Nutrition Scientist
Author of *The PRISE Life: Protein Pacing for Optimal Health and Performance*
www.paularciero.com

Having professional expertise is a true asset. Whether you've spent years in academia or decades honing your skills on the job, if you continually expand your knowledge and work with clients who benefit from your expertise, you have valuable insights to share. Writing a book is an effective way to convey your unique message to a broader audience. A book allows you to teach on paper instead of in person.

Consider Dr. Paul Arciero, an O'Leary Publishing author whose book transformed his professional life and the lives of his readers. Dr. Paul, a leading scientist in nutrition and applied physiology, has served as an expert for elite athletes and has authored over 70 peer-reviewed scientific papers.

He decided to distill his research into a book, making his insights accessible and actionable for the public. His book achieved a No. 1 new release in multiple categories and has not only been widely read since its publication a few years ago, but has also opened doors for him as a keynote speaker, consultant, and media personality – all while he continues his academic career.

Like Dr. Paul, you might possess academic or industry expertise that could greatly benefit others outside your immediate professional circle. Publishing a book allows you to share that knowledge more broadly, potentially transforming lives and enhancing your own career. Imagine the impact of bringing your specialized knowledge to the world! Writing a book could be the perfect way to do it!

❷ I have overcome some difficult personal circumstances that could inspire others.

Diana Ward, Mental Health Professional
Author of *Behind the Smile: The Heartbreaking Journey of Raising a Son with Mental Illness and Addiction*
www.dianawardauthor.com

Life brings challenges for everyone. Whether you have ended a difficult relationship, left a cult, gotten sober, lost a child, or faced some other difficult situation, human experiences can be transformed into meaningful and powerful lighthouses to help others navigate their lives.

Diana Ward, a dedicated mother and mental health professional, raised her three children with love, support, and compassion. Despite her diligent efforts, tragedy struck when her son, Cody, died by suicide. Heartbroken, and with her world shattered, Diana endured a mother's profound grief.

As part of her healing process, Diana chose to tell her story. Her goal was to support other parents navigating the challenges of raising children with mental illness and addiction. Sharing her experiences wasn't easy, but Diana is grateful she did. She regularly receives messages from readers who tell her how profoundly her book has touched their lives. Her book achieved a No. 1 ranking on Amazon as a new release in the Parenting Boys category. Through her writing, Diana ensures that Cody's legacy continues to make a difference.

Perhaps – like Diana – you've faced challenging experiences. Sharing your story can be incredibly powerful, and can offer hope and guidance to others in need. Never underestimate the impact of your story; it could be the beacon of light that guides someone out of darkness.

❸ I want to enhance my public speaking opportunities, professionally or personally.

Kendra Petty, Strategic Executive
Author of *I Can't Believe I'm Not Dead: Escaping Abuse, A Cult, Attempted Murder and Other Insanities ... A Story that Cannot Be True, But Is*
www.kendrapettyofficial.com

Have you ever imagined yourself in front of an audience, sharing your knowledge or a personal story? Do you have a knack for communication? Writing a book can open doors to new speaking opportunities – on stage, on podcasts, or in virtual settings.

Kendra Petty has been speaking as part of her high-powered career for decades. Yet her personal story was hidden behind closed doors… until now. Kendra decided it was time to share her hero's journey – which includes surviving abuse, the tragic loss of her brother in childhood, and leaving the cult her parents started. As if that's not enough, she also escaped attempted murder.

Her story is not just a "made-for-Hollywood movie" – it is her real life. She has truly overcome some impossible situations and has turned her personal tragedy into triumph. Now, she is elevating her message via the stage to inspire others to rise above their circumstances.

Writing a book can significantly boost your career by creating opportunities to speak at industry conferences. A book provides instant credibility; it can be more effective than almost any other work you could produce. By authoring a book, you can fast-track your way onto the stage, amplify your voice, and reach a wider audience.

Ultimately, you can help more people than you ever thought possible!

❹ I want to enhance or pivot in my career.

Karen Shepherd, HR Professional
Author of *Lead with Love: 10 Heart-Centered Strategies to Build a More Profitable Business*
www.hrbykaren.com

Attracting the right clients or standing out in a crowded market is a challenge many business owners face. Many opt for fancy websites, Google ads, or local networking to boost exposure. But imagine the positive impact publishing a book could have on your business!

Take Karen Shepherd, for example. She was already a recognized figure in southwest Florida and president of the local affiliate chapter of the Society for Human Resource Management (SHRM). She had earned awards like the Naples Community Choice and Business of the Month by the Greater Naples Chamber of Commerce. Still, she wondered how she could elevate her business even more. Her answer? Write a book.

Karen's book, *Lead with Love*, delves into 10 specific strategies for building a more profitable business that reflect her profound expertise in human resources and leadership. It quickly became a No. 1 new release on Amazon in the Business Health & Stress category. Not only has her book showcased her knowledge, but it has also been a powerful tool for attracting higher-tier clients. Her book is an especially beneficial for small to medium-sized businesses that lack a dedicated HR department and are most in need of her services, making it an excellent lead generation tool for HR by Karen. The launch party at her Naples, Florida office was a smashing success, drawing over 100 attendees.

If you're looking to elevate your career and draw a more distinguished clientele, consider writing a book. It's not just a marker of your expertise – it's an invitation to potential clients to see the value you can bring to their businesses. Writing a book is not just about book sales, it's about helping you achieve the professional goals you have as well.

❺ I want a strategic marketing tool for my career.

Jennifer Johnson, Owner, True Fashionistas and The Confident Entrepreneur
Author of *Grace & Grit: Becoming a Confident Entrepreneur*
www.truefashionistas.com and
www.jenniferannjohnson.com

In the dynamic world of entrepreneurship, sharing your journey through a book can significantly enhance your personal and professional brand. Whether you're running a thriving startup or leading a successful business enterprise, capturing the challenges and successes of your professional journey can inspire others. A book can also confirm your position as an industry expert. Your book not only serves as a testament to your resilience and innovation, but also opens new avenues for growth and opportunities.

Jennifer Johnson is a seasoned entrepreneur with a flair for marketing. Her retail store, True Fashionistas, has become the largest resale consignment shop in Florida. Drawing on her entrepreneurial successes, Jennifer decided to share her insights on building a business grounded in her core values of grace and grit to foster confidence and success.

She envisioned a practical book aimed at helping small business owners define their core values and then use them to build a strong foundation for future business growth. The book highlights her personal journey, including her failures and the challenges she overcame — obstacles that could have easily discouraged anyone. Following the launch of her book, which hit No. 1 on Amazon's new release list in the Retailing Industry category, Jennifer has continued to thrive.

For anyone growing a small business, writing a book can be a powerful marketing tool. It can enhance your brand's value and unlock new opportunities. Today, in addition to running True Fashionistas, Jennifer has launched The Confident Entrepreneur, a flourishing consulting business. She offers courses and coaching, along with speaking engagements and incorporates her book with all her offerings.

❻ I want to share professional lessons with future leaders.

C. Elliott Haverlack, Senior Executive and Change Agent Leader
Author of *Firestarter: Igniting Change Through Leadership*
www.cehaverlack.com

For many accomplished leaders, the idea of a leisurely retirement spent on the golf course or pickleball court doesn't quite hit the mark. These individuals thrive on continual engagement – helping others reach their potential and paving the way for future generations. If you have a proven track record in your field, along with the scars to show for it, why not share your wealth of knowledge with up-and-coming leaders?

That is exactly what Elliott has done. Having authored three books, he channels his wisdom through personal anecdotes and invaluable insights to impact new and developing leaders. His books include the timely letters he penned as a manager to his teams, providing regular encouragement and guidance.

While Elliott could easily while away his days, basking in the Florida sun or fishing for pike at Misaw Lake Lodge – an activity he enjoys from time to time – his passion to foster leadership burns fiercely. He continues to harness that passion by distilling decades of experience into writing. His knowledge and advice enable others to benefit from his 40-year journey in the consumer packaged goods industry.

Writing a book is not just an act of passion, but a profound act of generosity. The adage, "To whom much is given, much is required," resonates deeply with Elliott. His books are not only rich in guidance, but also equipped with practical tools that any aspiring leader would find invaluable.

❼ I am passionate about enhancing the visibility and impact of a nonprofit or cause.

Becky Savage, RN, Founder of the 525 Foundation
Author of *#ONECHOICE: How Ten Seconds Can Change Your Life*
www.525foundation.org

Having a passion is wonderful, and starting a nonprofit to channel that passion is even more impactful. But pairing that nonprofit with a book that educates others about its mission and importance can be transformative. That is the path Becky Savage took after tragically losing two of her sons, Nick and Jack, to accidental opioid overdoses on the same night.

In their memory, Becky established the 525 Foundation. Their mission is to save lives by being the catalyst for positive change in our schools, families, and communities. The 525 Foundation hosts fundraisers, awareness campaigns, and prescription drug drop-offs in Becky's community.

Because she wanted to make a direct impact on youth, Becky wrote her sons' story. Her book, *#ONECHOICE: How Ten Seconds Can Change Your Life*, launched as a No. 1 new release on Amazon in the Drug & Alcohol Abuse for Teens & Young Adults category. The book accompanies Becky when she speaks at schools across the United States. It is also used in classrooms, and teaches teens about the critical dangers of opioid use. The book drives home the message that even a single choice can be fatal.

If you, or someone you know, runs a nonprofit or is deeply committed to a cause, writing a book can significantly extend one's reach. It's a powerful way to share a story, educate others, raise awareness, and attract donations to a cause.

❽ I have a social media following and they are curious to know more.

Sarah Temima, Social Media Influencer
Author of *Can I Be Honest? The Distorted Path of Sex, Lies, and Healing*
Instagram @sarahtemima

Have you dedicated time and energy to growing your social media following and are now ready to monetize your hard work and share your origin story or inspiring message in depth? It's time to consider writing a book!

Your followers – friends, fans, and loyal supporters – form a ready-made audience. They already know, like, and trust you, and they're eager for more. Every like and comment on your posts, reels, and lives is a testament to their interest. Why not give them more of what they crave?

Take Sarah Temima, for example. As an Instagram influencer, Sarah grew her following to over 200,000 fans while portraying a luxurious, globe-trotting lifestyle. Yet, realizing the disconnect between her online persona and her reality, she chose to reveal the truth about her life in her book, *Can I Be Honest?*

Through her candid narrative, she shared her highs and lows – the good, the bad, and the ugly. Now a mother, Sarah lives a life rooted in honesty. Her book has encouraged her followers to question the glossy veneer of social media and to embrace authenticity.

If you have a social media following, an email list, or any large network of people who value your voice, it's time to offer them more of you. Writing a book can deepen your connection with your audience in a meaningful way. Why not give it a shot?

❾ I want to inspire others along their spiritual journey.

Thomas Hudson, MD, Diagnostic Radiologist
Author of *Something Deeper: 31 Spiritual Poems to Help You Navigate Life*
www.thomashudsonmd.com

What if you simply want to write a book about something that is unrelated to your profession? We encourage you to go for it! Writing a book can be a transformational experience that leads to a profound understanding of yourself and the world around you. Through sharing your insights, you can inspire others too. This was precisely the approach taken by Thomas Hudson, MD, in his book *Something Deeper: 31 Spiritual Poems to Help You Navigate Life.*

Dr. Hudson, a diagnostic radiologist with over 40 years of experience, has witnessed the fragility of life through a unique lens. From offering reassurance to patients with benign mammograms to navigating the delicate process of delivering cancer diagnoses, he has experienced the spectrum of human emotion. These profound encounters prompted him to explore his own spirituality, leading him to write spiritual poetry that he formerly just shared via email with some close friends and family. The positive response he received over decades of sharing led him to decide to publish his poetry publicly. He feels this has been one of the most impactful projects of his life.

Today, while continuing his practice and offering telehealth consultations, Dr. Hudson finds that the humanity he shares with his patients – along with the depth of his spiritual writings – has not only aided his personal growth but also brings peace to others during challenging times.

If you possess a rich intellectual or spiritual life and wish to share your experiences through poetry, prose, or personal stories of hope, writing a book could be one of the most fulfilling endeavors you undertake. It's a project that promises lasting impact, extending well beyond the confines of emails and journal entries.

❿ I want to leave a legacy for future generations.

Winston Williams, Writer/Photographer
Author of *Under a Cloud of Sails: Memoirs of a Free Spirit*
www.olearypublishing.com/books

No One Gets Out of Here Alive isn't just a biography of Jim Morrison, the iconic lead singer of the Doors; it echoes the inevitable truth that we all face – eventually, each of us will have a last day. Take a moment to reflect on the life you've lived and the lessons you've learned thus far. What adventures have defined you? What wisdom would you impart to your family, friends and future generations? What might you say to help them lead happier, more fulfilling lives? What pitfalls do you hope they will avoid, and how?

That kind of thinking was the inspiration behind Winston "Win" Williams' memoir, *Under a Cloud of Sails*. Win wasn't famous or wealthy, but he was an adventurer who had sailed the world on a tall ship. He dove into the depths of alcoholism and miraculously survived. He had the opportunity to write and photograph for National Geographic and became a ship's captain himself. A decade before we met Win he had tried to attract the attention of a traditional publisher, with no luck. Now in his 80s, with his 70,000 word manuscript lying dormant on his bookshelf, Win was certain his book was never going to see the light of day. Luckily, this story has a happy ending! We were able to resurrect his manuscript and publish his book including many photos from his adventures. He was able to tell his story, in his own words, and he enjoyed a large book signing with hundreds of friends in attendance.

Winston passed away less than a year after publishing his memoir, with over 40 years of sobriety. His book *Under a Cloud of Sails* is a legacy treasured by his four children and a growing tree of grandchildren and great-grandchildren.

Do you want your stories to linger with family and friends after you're gone? What do you want to be remembered for? Overcoming challenges? Achieving goals? Or, perhaps you'd like to leave a spiritual legacy? Whatever your reason is, now is the time to put your life's story on paper. Only you can narrate your experiences with true authenticity. Winston's story continues to resonate – will yours?

Exercise: What is your WHY?

Turn back to page 5 and look at the statements you circled – those "YES" answers are your reasons to write your book. Whether you want to share your professional expertise, inspire others with your personal triumphs, or accelerate your business growth, your motivation is valid. Your WHY could be altruistic, capitalistic, or a mix of both. What matters is that you clearly define your core reason WHY you want to write a book. Take a moment to complete this exercise to dig below the surface and find your deeper why. This happens by asking WHY multiple times to uncover what is truly important to you.

I want to write a book about:

_____

_____

because _____

_____

_____

Why is this important?

_____

_____

And why is that important?

_____

_____

And why is that important?

_____

_____

And why is that important?

_____

_____

Keep digging until you feel that core reason in your soul. Maybe you will tear up, or you'll get goose bumps, or you'll feel butterflies in your stomach. Perhaps you'll feel a sense of urgency. You will know that you were made for such a time as this!

Each of the 10 authors you just met had a deep reason for writing their book; a reason that is personal to them. The surface reason is what helped them start the process; the core reason is why they completed it!

Write your core WHY below:

I want to write a book about
_____
because _____
_____
_____

Imagine if you could accomplish this tangible project and realize its impact in the world. How does that feel? Circle the emotions below that describe this feeling inside of you.

Triumphant	Fulfilled	Proud	Elated
Empowered	Inspired	Satisfied	Motivated
Committed	Grateful	Optimistic	Relieved
Accomplished	Energized	Confident	Valued
Recognized	Respected	Renewed	Jubilant

Smile. You can do this. Now let's talk about HOW!

PART
(2)

But How?

Now that we have covered ten compelling reasons to embark on the author's journey and identified your unique WHY, we are now poised to dive into the HOW. Let's embark on an exciting exploration of transforming your unique idea into a published book. This is where your vision starts to take shape, turning inspiration into a tangible reality that can be shared with the world.

From Idea to Manuscript

Transforming your idea into a manuscript is both exhilarating and challenging. It's a creative journey that is unlike anything you might have accomplished before. As you craft each sentence and structure every chapter, you'll not only be shaping a book, but also refining your thoughts and delivering them to your future readers with confidence. This process is as rewarding as it is rigorous, offering you a unique opportunity to express yourself and make a lasting impact. The good news is… you do not have to do it alone!

Not everyone is cut out for the keyboard. If you're more visionary than scribe, consider working with a ghostwriter. A ghostwriter is someone who will help you structure your message into an outline and then record interviews with you over a period of time. They will write on your behalf, using your words and your stories. This is a great way to delegate the writing process to someone who is a skilled writer while preserving your time to continue working in your area of expertise. At O'Leary Publishing, we often provide ghostwriting services for our busy professional clients and those who prefer to outsource the writing of their book. It's a great option for anyone who wants to be a published author and is open to delegating the writing to someone else.

For those who prefer a more hands-on approach, working with a developmental editor while you write your book may be the right path for you. Our editors provide structured support to keep you focused. From crafting an outline to maintaining a clear vision and continuity with your back cover summary, they will guide you every step of the way. With this process you'll be able to stay focused on your reader and your book's message without getting lost in the details. Writing isn't about sporadic bursts of inspiration – it's about consistency. If you are writing your book yourself, aim to write daily. Even 500 words a day quickly adds up, helping to build momentum and refine your craft. Remember, rough drafts are just that – rough. The key is to keep writing.

Whether you choose to work with a ghostwriter or an editorial team, you must remember that every writer creating a book benefits from collaboration. Our team at O'Leary Publishing will support you from first draft to final page, ensuring that your book progresses from a dream to a deadline-driven reality.

Completing your manuscript is just one part of becoming an author. Creating a marketing plan, identifying your audience, and having a strategy for the book launch are crucial. It is essential to position your book for maximum impact in the marketplace.

Always remember, perfection isn't the goal; completion is. Write the best manuscript you can, work with your editorial team and breathe. You can do it!

From Manuscript to Publication

Publishing a book is an exciting endeavor, and choosing the right team is crucial. O'Leary Publishing, a hybrid book publishing company based in Naples, Florida, is ready to make your dream of authoring a book a reality! We work with aspiring authors all across the United States, offering a full-service team of editors and designers who deliver high-quality books that can compete with traditionally published books.

You'll work closely with a dedicated project manager who will guide you through every stage of production. Our comprehensive service includes a personalized publishing timeline and a skilled editorial team. We provide custom interior layouts and cover designs, moving away from the template-based approaches of many other publishers.

We also offer a marketing strategy session to help you define your specific goals for your book and create a plan to reach those goals. Our post-publishing support includes organizing a successful book launch, developing a PR/media packet, and creating author-branded websites and social media accounts when needed. These efforts often lead our authors to achieve No. 1 new release status on Amazon in their first week.

Our project cycles vary from six to twelve months, tailored to your needs. After the book launch, we continue to support our authors with promotional help and a generous royalty program to maximize your return on investment. Additionally, we provide opportunities for our authors to speak at our annual Booked Naples event. Remember that uncovering your WHY and understanding HOW can unleash the tremendous potential within you.

Whether your motivation to write springs from your professional expertise, personal triumphs, or a desire to inspire or lead, your journey holds valuable lessons for others.

Perhaps you're aiming to increase your public speaking opportunities, pivot in your career, or leverage your book as a strategic marketing tool. Maybe your goal is to raise awareness, and more money, for your nonprofit, engage your social media followers on a deeper level, or guide others on their spiritual path. Whatever the reason, it is your WHY that matters most.

We believe every book published contributes to the rich tapestry of human experience and has the power to enlighten, inspire, and influence humanity. By writing your book, you are not just sharing knowledge – you are crafting a legacy that will inform and inspire future generations.

How to Get Started

Choosing a publishing partner is a major decision for any author. At O'Leary Publishing, we understand the importance of each book. We do our utmost to return the trust authors place in us by delivering the highest-quality services available anywhere. Choose from one of the following two options to get started today.

Complete the Author Adventure Quiz Online

At O'Leary Publishing, we believe it is important to go into any publishing partnership with eyes wide open. That is why we have created a free 10 question Author Adventure Quiz online. You already answered 1 of the 10 questions on page 5, now go and answer the other 9 to see if you are ready to adventure towards authorship. If you haven't done so already, please scan the code on the next page to be taken directly to the quiz.

Schedule a Publishing Consultation

If you have already taken the quiz and you are ready to start your publishing journey it is time to chat with someone on our team. We will answer any questions you may have and ask some strategic questions about your book, so that we can recommend the best publishing experience for you.

Now it's your turn! Choose one QR code below and scan it now.

Scan to Take   Scan to Schedule
the Quiz   a Consultation

After you are done scanning one of the two codes, please go on to Part 3.

PART

(3)

Who, Me?
Yes, You!

Stephen Covey, the celebrated author of *The 7 Habits of Highly Effective People,* once said, "The most significant things you'll do in life are not urgent, but they are important." Imagine if Covey had never shared his insights! Writing a book embodies Covey's principle – it's a significant, profound, life-altering task that's too easily deferred indefinitely. If not now, when? If not you, who? Don't allow the anonymous THEYs to discourage you from sharing the story, the experience, the expertise that only you can share.

Take the leap and embark on this meaningful journey today. Create something that will endure long after you've moved on to your next adventure. Envision the satisfaction of walking into a business meeting and presenting your book as a gift to a potential client. Picture your name next to a glowing No. 1 new release badge on Amazon. Imagine the messages from readers whose lives your book has changed. This isn't just a fantasy; it's an achievable reality.

Don't let procrastination diminish your potential impact. Remember, authors like Karen Shepherd, Jennifer Johnson, Sarah Temima, Elliott Haverlack, Dr. Thomas Husdon, Diana Ward, Dr. Paul Arciero, Becky Savage, Kendra Petty, and Winston 'Win' Williams, who all started with a simple idea, a personal experience, or a burning passion. They took the necessary steps to share their messages with the world, and so can YOU.

Today, stop questioning, "Who, me? An author?" and start affirming, "Yes, me! An author!" Now is the time to act. The fact that you've read to the end of this book is no coincidence – it's your *sign from the universe*. We're here to support you as you turn your vision into reality. Don't close this book without committing to take your first step. We're ready to guide you on your exciting Author Adventure!

About
the Author

April O'Leary is the founder of O'Leary Publishing, a hybrid book publishing company located in Naples, Florida that supports professionals in creating books that educate, entertain, and inspire. April's unique approach assists authors in integrating their publications with their existing services, enhancing both their reach and influence. She is also a keynote speaker and author.

April orchestrates the annual Booked Naples event, a TEDx-style event that highlights the work of the O'Leary Publishing family of authors. She also hosts the I'm Booked Podcast, where she discusses the nuances of book publishing with authors, publishers, and industry experts, providing guidance to those eager to begin their writing journey.

Since its inception in 2019, O'Leary Publishing has been committed to the growth and success of its authors. Outside of her professional life, April is a dedicated mother to three daughters and resides in Naples, Florida. For more about April visit her personal website at apriloleary.com.

Made in the USA
Columbia, SC
18 February 2025